When to WALK AWAY After INFIDELITY

10 Signs to Understand When to Stay or Leave after Betrayal

How to Break Free from the Shackles of Infidelity and Find Your Path to Healing and Happiness

Author:
Blair Parker, Ph.D.

The pain and confusion can be overwhelming in the wake of infidelity. But within the chaos lies an opportunity for healing and growth. In this book, I, Blair Parker, Ph.D., a seasoned psychologist specializing in infidelity recovery, will guide you through understanding when to walk away and find your path to healing and happiness.

- Blair Parker -

DISCLAIMER

© Copyright 2023

All rights reserved. This book may not be reproduced or transmitted in any form, electronic, mechanical, photocopy, recording, or otherwise, without the author's permission. It is illegal to copy this book, post it to a website, or distribute it by any other means without permission.

Neither the publisher nor the author is engaged in rendering legal or any other professional service through this book. If expert assistance is required, the services of appropriate professionals should be sought. The publisher and the author shall have neither liability nor responsibility to any person or entity concerning any loss or damage caused directly or indirectly by the professional using the information in this book.

- **_About the Author: Blair Parker, Ph.D._**
- **_Introduction_**
- **_Chapter 0: Knowing When to Walk Away After Infidelity_** - _10 Signs to Understand_
- **_Chapter 1: The Whirlwind of Emotions: Understanding the Pain of Infidelity_**
  - Unveiling the Turmoil Within Navigating the Emotional Roller Coaster
  - Exploring the range of emotions experienced after infidelity
  - Guiding in managing and processing these emotions
  - Validating your feelings and reassuring you that you're not alone
  - Finding Solace and Validation in Your Feelings
  - Identifying the significance of validating your emotions
  - Offering techniques for seeking solace and support during this challenging time
  - Encouraging self-compassion and nurturing your emotional well-being

- ***Chapter 2: To Mend or End: The Power of Decision-Making After Infidelity***
  - Embracing the Complexity of Choosing Your Path Forward
  - Acknowledging the weight of the decision to stay or leave
  - Encouraging self-reflection and understanding personal values
  - Providing a framework to help you make an informed decision aligned with your well-being
  - Empowering Yourself to Make a Decision Aligned with Your Well-being
  - Breaking free from societal expectations and external pressures
  - Empowering you to trust your intuition and prioritize your happiness
  - Offering practical tools to aid in decision-making and creating a plan for your future

- **_Chapter 3: Unloving the Unfaithful: Rebuilding Trust and Self-Worth_**
  - Reclaiming Your Sense of Self Amidst Betrayal
  - Rediscovering your identity beyond the pain of infidelity
  - Restoring self-esteem and rebuilding self-worth
  - Nurturing self-care practices to promote healing and personal growth
  - Rediscovering Your Worth and Creating Boundaries for Healing
  - Setting healthy boundaries to protect yourself from further harm
  - Rebuilding trust in yourself and your judgment
  - Establishing boundaries within the relationship to foster healing and rebuild trust
  - HEALING MINDSET AFTER AN AFFAIR

- ***Chapter 4: When Words Are Empty: Signs of Genuine Remorse and Healing***
  - Deciphering Empty Promises from Authentic Accountability
  - Identifying the signs of genuine remorse and commitment to change
  - Understanding the impact of actions over words in the healing process
  - Guiding in establishing open and honest communication with your partner
  - Recognizing the Actions That Truly Reflect Remorse and Commitment to Change
  - Evaluating your partner's behavior for consistent change and growth
  - Highlighting key indicators of genuine remorse and commitment
  - Encouraging open dialogue and shared responsibility for rebuilding the relationship

- ***Chapter 5: Counseling as a Lifeline: Reconnecting and Communicating After Infidelity***
  - The Transformative Power of Professional Guidance
  - Exploring the benefits of seeking professional help in infidelity recovery
  - Finding the right therapist and understanding different therapeutic approaches
  - Emphasizing the importance of active participation in counseling sessions
  - Uncovering Effective Communication Strategies and Rebuilding Intimacy
  - Enhancing communication skills to promote understanding and empathy
  - Rebuilding intimacy through open and honest dialogue
  - Exploring techniques to strengthen emotional and physical connections
  - HEALING POWER OF GRATITUDE AFTER THE BETRAYAL

- ***Chapter 6: The Breaking Point: Recognizing When Efforts No Longer Suffice***
  - Navigating the Threshold of Exhaustion and Self-Care
  - Recognizing signs of emotional and physical exhaustion
  - Prioritizing self-care to regain strength and clarity
  - Understanding the importance of setting boundaries to protect your well-being
  - Acknowledging Your Limits and Reevaluating the Direction of Your Relationship
  - Reflecting on the progress made and evaluating if it aligns with your expectations
  - Recognizing when efforts to rebuild the relationship are no longer sufficient
  - Guiding you through the process of reevaluating your needs and considering alternative paths
  - WHEN I'M SURE THAT I WANT A DIVORCE

- ***Chapter 7: Severing Ties: Letting Go of Third-Party Connections for Good***
  - Understanding the Impact of Continued Contact on Healing
  - Examining the influence of third-party connections on the healing process
  - Addressing the complexities of cutting ties with those involved in the infidelity
  - Guiding creating boundaries and minimizing external influences
  - Embracing Closure and Cutting Off Unhealthy Attachments
  - Recognizing the importance of closure for moving forward
  - Strategies for letting go of toxic relationships and attachments
  - Cultivating a supportive network to aid in the healing process
  - ENDING ALL CONTACT
  - IF YOU WORK WITH THE AFFAIR PARTNER

- ***Chapter 8: The Stagnant Journey: Assessing Progress in the Relationship***
  - Evaluating the Signs of Growth or Stagnation in Post-Infidelity Recovery
  - Identifying indicators of progress and growth in the relationship
  - Addressing potential roadblocks that hinder forward movement
  - Offering guidance on effective communication and conflict resolution
  - Cultivating a Dynamic and Evolving Relationship Based on Mutual Commitment
  - Nurturing a relationship that embraces change and growth
  - Encouraging mutual commitment and shared responsibility for rebuilding trust
  - Fostering a supportive and nurturing partnership
  - PRACTICAL EXAMPLES OF EXERCISES AND ACTIVITIES FOR ASSESSING PROGRESS IN POST-INFIDELITY RECOVERY

- ***Chapter 9: Unbalanced Commitment: Sharing the Burden of Rebuilding***
  - Recognizing the Importance of Equal Effort in Healing
  - Discussing the significance of balanced commitment in the recovery process
  - Identifying signs of unequal effort and addressing imbalances
  - Strategies for fostering mutual commitment and active participation
  - Establishing Mutual Responsibility and Reinforcing Commitment
  - Building a solid foundation of trust and accountability
  - Promoting transparency and open communication within the relationship
  - Encouraging joint efforts in rebuilding and strengthening the bond
  - PROMOTING TRANSPARENCY

- ### _Chapter 10: Protecting Innocence: Children, Conflict, and the Decision to Leave_

  - Navigating the Challenging Terrain of Parenthood and Separation
  - Exploring the Impact of Infidelity on Children and parenting dynamics
  - Offering guidance on shielding children from conflict and fostering a healthy environment
  - Weighing the decision to leave against the potential effects on children
  - Prioritizing the Well-being of Children in the Context of a Troubled Relationship
  - Providing strategies for co-parenting and maintaining a supportive environment
  - Understanding when separation may be necessary for the well-being of all involved
  - Supporting children through the process of healing and adjustment
  - PROTECTING INNOCENCE

- ***Chapter 11: The Intimacy Dilemma: Rediscovering Physical Connection***
  - Healing Wounds and Rebuilding Intimacy in the Aftermath of Betrayal
  - Addressing challenges and fears, rebuilding physical intimacy
  - Tools and techniques for fostering emotional and physical connection
  - Promoting a safe and supportive space for vulnerability and healing
  - Fostering a Safe Space for Vulnerability and Rediscovering Physical Intimacy
  - Cultivating trust and mutual respect in rebuilding physical intimacy
  - Navigating past traumas and fears to embrace vulnerability
  - Encouraging open communication and exploration of desires and boundaries
  - REDISCOVERING COUPLE PHYSICAL CONNECTION POST-BETRAYAL
  - REDISCOVERING ONE'S BODY AND DESIRES IN CASE THE RELATIONSHIP ENDS

- ***Chapter 12: Trust Lost, Truth Elusive: Dealing with Deceit and Patterns of Dishonesty***
    - Breaking Free from the Cycle of Lies and Deception
    - Recognizing patterns of deceit and addressing them head-on
    - Strategies for rebuilding trust through transparency and honesty
    - Promoting a culture of truthfulness and integrity within the relationship
    - Rebuilding Trust Through Transparency and Accountability
    - Establishing mechanisms for accountability and rebuilding

- ***SPECIAL BONUS CHAPTER: Managing the Financial Aspects after Divorce***:
  Navigating a New Financial Landscape

- ***SECOND SPECIAL BONUS CHAPTER:***
  - *What to do when it's time to walk away after an affair*
  - *Your future without help from your partner*

- ***Conclusion: Embracing Your Path to Healing***
  - Reflecting on the Transformational Journey of Healing and Growth
  - Embracing a Future Filled with Empowerment and Possibilities

About the Author

With over 15 years of experience as a psychologist specializing in infidelity dynamics within relationships, Blair Parker has become recognized for her comprehensive insights into these often complex issues. She brings compassion and resilience-building strategies when assisting individuals and couples on their road toward recovery from emotional wounds inflicted by betrayals committed therein. Dr.Parker offers tailored services based on each client's unique journey because she believes every individual deserves personalized attention and genuine care during this adversity-riddled process, which requires immense courage; it also demands insightful psychological knowledge - something Dr.Parker certainly possesses! Dr.Blair Parker is one of the industry's most exceptional professionals in helping couples and individuals recover from infidelity trauma - thanks to her warm and personable nature and professional expertise that allows people to open up to her quickly.

Dr.Parker has garnered significant recognition over the years for working as an author and speaker, dedicatedly sharing insights based on personal experiences counseling those impacted by infidelity's ramifications. Countless publications regularly feature articles highlighting this expert psychologist's unique approach to healing-related matters, which have earned admiration from reputable sources across different mediums internationally. With credentials like these underlining her professional profile, it is no surprise that global conferences and workshops frequently clamor for Dr. Parkers's speaking engagements on such matters.

Beyond work, though - nothing gives this compassionate woman more joy than spending time outdoors or traveling with family while discovering new cultures worldwide. The objective of this individual is to facilitate her clients in seizing hold of their journey toward recovery and fashioning a future brimming with love, trust, and genuine joy.

Introduction

Welcome to "When to Walk Away after Infidelity". This guidebook provides practical advice, support, and encouragement explicitly designed for those tackling the rough terrain of infidelity. We will unravel the intricate processes tied to restoring trust while fostering opportunities for empowerment.

Infidelity is an incredibly personal topic that has far-reaching effects on people's lives and relationships: Sensitive handling through empathy and a nonjudgmental approach are invaluable traits when addressing this subject. Our main goal is to provide a compassionate environment where you can explore your emotions without any constraints while developing all the necessary tools to help you achieve optimal growth.

My name is Blair- having gone through one myself, I understand how challenging navigating infidelity can be fully well! By sharing my journey alongside vital lessons learned throughout it all, I sincerely hope that others grappling with similar circumstances might find solace in knowing they aren't alone. The fundamental goal of this book is to provide practical assistance and guidance while navigating the aftermath of infidelity in one's life. The aim is for readers to feel empowered by encouraging self-reflection while making informed decisions concerning their well-being.

Exploring various topics related to healing from infidelities, such as rebuilding trust and creating a future filled with love, confidence, and happiness.

This guide distinguishes itself by providing specific strategies grounded through real-life examples that go beyond traditional resources on infidelity, with general concepts only available elsewhere. Offering actionable steps aimed at helping readers overcome hurdles encountered throughout their journey toward recovery provides comprehensive guidance acknowledging difficulties inherent within relationships.

I aspire that this book offers significant value in one's quest for healing from infidelity; therefore, I urge readers always approach its content with an open mind focused on reflection. Reflecting upon presented ideas will help readers discover how to utilize these insights to address their unique challenges. The healing process after infidelity is not an easy journey - it takes time, effort, patience, and kindness toward oneself. Nonetheless, one must remember that they are not alone in their quest towards recovery; this ultimate guide provides a comprehensive set of tools upon which one can rebuild trust while embracing personal growth for long-term empowerment and happiness beyond just surviving such challenging experiences. May readers find meaningful insights within these pages as we wish them strength and guidance throughout their journey.

Chapter 0: Knowing When to Walk Away After Infidelity - 10 Signs to Understand

When faced with infidelity within a relationship deciding whether or not to stay can be an arduous task demanding careful consideration and introspection. Understanding when walking away is necessary can empower you but can prove challenging. Here we have compiled ten signs that may help guide your decision-making process.

1. Your partner shows no remorse for their betrayal: One clear indication of undervaluing a relationship is lacking sincere remorse after betraying one's partner. Words hold little meaning without matching actions; their inability or unwillingness to acknowledge their wrongdoing and take responsibility suggests little chance of improvement for your connection.

2. They refuse counseling as a couple: Communication serves as a foundation of relationships while therapy promotes healing

post-infidelity, which is particularly critical in such situations; if your spouse declines couple counseling or working on problems together, it hints at lacking initiative in repairing or addressing marital issues.

3. Exhaustion from constantly trying to fix the relationship: Healing takes time and effort - infidelity can slice deep into the soul. It may be time to reconsider if you continue to feel exhausted as if running on empty when trying to mend your bond. If all efforts at fixing a relationship fall squarely on your shoulders while your partner remains unresponsive or indifferent, it may signify that you've hit rock bottom. Once you no longer care about receiving apologies or not, this indicates that all your patience has worn thin. Moreover, even if remorse is expressed sincerely by one's partner who also seeks counseling, maintaining ties with the person they cheated on undermines any attempt at rebuilding trust, which can leave

you feeling quite uncertain. It's worth bearing in mind, too, that repairing relationships post-infidelity is an uphill struggle requiring

equal dedication from both parties to make any headway. Without visible positive change along the way accompanied by genuine efforts by each other,

the experience can turn out quite disappointing - especially when faced with no growth whatsoever. It will examine whether settling for such stagnation in a relationship is worthwhile.

Lastly, it's important to remember that healing and rebuilding trust should involve both partners;

when one person bears all the weight of healing alone, it inevitably creates friction and diminishes the chances of progress. When one person has to accept all the responsibility for repairing a broken relationship, it indicates an imbalance and lack of commitment from their partner. Both partners must invest equal effort into healing to succeed together. It requires cooperation in rebuilding lost trust or connection.

Although considering our children's well-being may seem logical, staying in an unhappy or loveless marriage can have dire consequences on them long-term as they are often more attuned than we give them credit for. Their emotional intelligence could sense tension or unhappiness emanating from our marital discord; thus, prioritizing their psychological health by creating a helpful environment will keep everyone happy. A significant barrier to rebuilding lost trust and connection is when physical intimacy becomes non-existent. It takes time and patience to restore this aspect of marriage, but a persistent absence of physical intimacy may indicate it might be too late for us to salvage things. Trust is the fundamental pillar of any healthy relationship; that's why continuous dishonesty can erode over time.

Repeated deception makes it challenging for couples to recover or rebuild the lost foundation making honesty the only way to build or promote a positive marital connection. When your partner consistently lies and deceives you, trusting anything they say becomes challenging. Continuing in a relationship where trust has been repeatedly broken can have disastrous consequences for your emotional well-being.

Even after trying everything - therapy sessions traveling together, rebuilding intimacy - if the deep pain and sense of betrayal don't go away, perhaps it's best to call it quits. Sometimes wounds from unfaithfulness go too far down to heal entirely with good intentions or efforts alone.

Remember that both partners have roles in keeping the marriage together - yet sometimes cheating is the catalyst that shows that further effort is futile. If finding happiness within this connection seems impossible or cannot move past feelings caused by cheating- considering divorce and starting anew might best serve everyone involved.

Deciding whether to leave or stay in an adulterous relationship is extraordinarily personal, requiring careful consideration between two individuals before deciding what's best. Dealing with an affair's aftermath can be incredibly challenging - full of complex emotions and pain. Understanding when it's time to move on takes considerable thought and self-awareness; however, making such a decision can provide strength and empowerment too. This article will explore ten signs indicating when you should release yourself from the situation. One crucial sign might be your partner's lack of authentic remorse for their betrayal. Ignoring or failing, even just acknowledging how much they've hurt you, implies that repairing things may not be possible without a willingness on both sides and words alone being insufficient measures.

Also important is whether your spouse seeks marital counseling geared toward reconciliation. In any partnership, open communication remains vital - particularly after infidelity. Avoiding therapy sessions or failing to address root issues could mean more profound ones requiring attention.

It's understandable if you're exhausted and working hard to resolve the situation without progress. The wounds caused by infidelity run deep and linger long after apologies have been made. With time emotions often become dull leading to apathy which signals a lack of emotional endurance. Learning when to back out of a hurtful situation allows us better chances of finding happiness and peace. Some people find holding onto past relationships complex, even under trying circumstances. The inability of one party involved in not committing enough effort shows an unwillingness to fix what is broken. It's up to the affected partner to decide if the relationship has reached a point of no return. It takes commitment from both partners to rebuild trust and restore a breached bond following infidelity. If one party isn't making an effort, it could mean they are not fully invested in repairing things between you two.

When children are involved in this complicated equation deciding whether or not to end, things might become even more complex for you as a couple. However, sticking together for your kids might seem right at first glance. Exposing them constantly to toxic situations can have severe psychological implications that must be considered carefully.

Physical intimacy plays an essential role in restoring trust and connection after cheating. However, it only works when there's still mutual desire between partners - if that's no longer there, unfortunately, what's been broken may now be beyond repair.

A pattern of dishonesty or infidelity indicates a fundamental breakdown of trust that cannot be fixed quickly or easily. While cheating may seem isolated initially, it can eventually become a recurring behavior pattern that damages one's character permanently over time. It can also create lasting emotional damage—living with constant worry and suspicion creates significant implications for overall health and mental stability.

Therefore prioritizing our overall wellness involves removing ourselves from relationships where integrity remains questionable repeatedly for sustained periods. Sometimes even if we do our best to overcome betrayal, the pain inflicted by unfaithfulness may continue to affect us profoundly for an extended period making it essential to let go for greater peace of mind.

While these ten signs provide valuable guidance about when it might be time to walk away after experiencing infidelity, remember each person has their unique journey with its challenges requiring custom solutions rather than a one size fits all approach dictated by any sole set of strict guidelines or rules irrespective of how useful they are nonetheless. Infidelity causes tremendous pain and turmoil that demands careful thoughtfulness before deciding anything related.

Trusting your senses while identifying emotions is essential when making big decisions during catastrophic events like cheating on significant others. This book explores ten warning signs associated with infidelity recovery while delving into various viewpoints around this subject matter in depth across the twelve chapters within it - we provide practical solutions to navigate the complexities involved when rebuilding trust following betrayal-driven relationship breakdowns.

By reading through each chapter carefully- individuals struggling through afflictions linked to infidelity can gain insights and learn new tools and essential strategies needed to rebuild trust after being hurt by their partners. Our goal is to offer comprehensive guidance that addresses emotional, psychological, and practical aspects of healing with empathy and respect for each person's unique circumstances without leaving anything out.

Finally, I appreciate my competitors' work on Amazon in this sphere and their contributions to the broader conversation around people's deeply personal yet profoundly challenging experiences dealing with infidelity.

As we embark on this critical journey together, I'd like us to explore these signs in greater detail - delving deep into their complexities to understand better how they relate to our individual experiences when coping with infidelity in our friendships or relationships.

By gaining insight into these symptoms, we can mentally equip ourselves for what lies ahead, learning how best to prepare ourselves emotionally so as not to let negativity around our experience tear us down but instead rise more robust than ever!

Throughout subsequent chapters, I'll provide practical advice for healing from past wounds and rebuilding trust lost during moments of vulnerability resulting from unfaithfulness or deceitful behavior by those closest to us.

Each chapter includes personal anecdotes and exercises explicitly tailored towards supporting readers through difficult times towards growth and renewal. Prioritizing your well-being while trusting your intuition is critical in achieving healing.

Remember that you are strong enough to overcome this difficult chapter in your life, and there's optimism for a better future despite experiencing betrayal's pain.

Explore Chapter 1 - Reflecting on the Transformational Journey of Healing and Growth - where we delve into the early stages of recovery by reflecting on oneself.

Chapter 1: The Whirlwind of Emotions: Understanding the Pain of Infidelity

As you hold onto this book, I can feel your emotions stirring within. Infidelity cuts deep, making wounds that may hurt too much to heal. You may feel uncertain about yourself while losing trust in others around you and questioning your self-worth.

But don't worry; we'll embark on a journey towards finding yourself again - healing and happiness will occur. In this chapter, we explore the many emotions associated with infidelity, such as pain and confusion, while validating each so that no piece goes untouched.

When dealing with such situations, the emotional landscape is difficult for anyone. Understanding it is essential since it will help clarify what lies ahead, including navigating future challenges smartly based on prior experiences.

Turbulent Emotions: Guiding You Through Your Emotional Roller Coaster

Infidelity sets off an emotional roller coaster that throws everything into chaos, including anger, sadness, disbelief, and betrayal like waves crashing upon your heart. During such trying times of infidelity, acknowledge and accept every emotion that arises for proper healing. Allow yourself to feel the anger surging through your veins while recognizing the profound loss and sadness accompanying this event.

It's usually during these moments to question whether your emotions are valid or perhaps an overreaction or being too sensitive about irrelevant issues. But don't worry- know what you feel is justified, dear reader!

Take comfort in trusted family members or friends who lend an ear and offer compassion when needed. Sharing one's story is a release from carrying heavy emotional weights alone while finding validation in others who've experienced similar things –always remember, You're never alone! In light of infidelity, individuals commonly experience internal struggles such as self-blame and shame - emotions that run deep and are difficult to navigate alone.

Before delving into these issues further, it is essential to understand that there's no right or wrong way to feel during this healing process from betrayal- be kind towards yourself when things get tough.

As you journey through the upcoming chapters, we will explore the underbelly of self-blame by understanding how one could feel responsible for their partner's actions and bear guilt unfairly due to internalized shame.

By working through these complex emotions together, we could cultivate self-compassion, which is essential in nurturing our bruised self-esteem.

We must embrace this journey toward healing as an ongoing process rather than expecting it all at once without any bumps on the road.

During infidelity, finding comfort through support is critical to healing. Opening up to trusted friends or family members lends an empathetic ear toward the situation; additionally, joining support groups creates an environment where others understand similar experiences providing valuable coping mechanisms for addressing distressful situations.

Lastly, seeking professional help from licensed therapists equips individuals with the correct tools to manage complicated emotions while navigating this challenging time. Here are some practical ways individuals can receive solace and assistance during these difficult moments:

1) Trustworthy Friend/Family Sharing - Confide with someone who cares about you profoundly and allows options for emotional safety nets

2) Support Groups - Involvement within communal groups allows those experiencing similar scenarios to offer beneficial advice and support.

3) Professional Help - An individual will gain insight into various coping mechanisms for managing stress and anxiety during this challenging time with licensed therapists.

4) Self-Care Focus - Prioritizing self-care, including exercise, meditation, or journaling techniques, is essential. These activities keep mental and physical health in check. Overcoming infidelity within a partnership is a difficult journey that requires one to be patient with themselves and dedicate the resources necessary for proper recovery.

5) It's essential to allow the range of emotions that arise in response to infidelity into your consciousness, even if they may seem objectionable or raw at times- stifling them only impedes progress.

6) Mindfulness techniques like deep breathing exercises or guided meditation can help calm anxiety during this transitional period.

7) Couples therapy can also help rebuild trust and repair relationships damaged by betrayal over time if both parties are open to it. Be kind and compassionate with yourself during this challenging period- you will come out on the other side stronger for it.

While recovering from infidelity may seem impossible at times, this book reminds us that there is always hope for healing. Its practical tools and sincere support offer readers a path toward rediscovering themselves post-betrayal.

Together we will navigate the complexities of this journey - dismantling layers of pain to emerge with newfound strength and wisdom on the other side. Wishing you all the best as you embark upon this transformative reading experience!

Chapter 2: To Mend or End: The Power of Decision-Making After Infidelity

Embracing the Complexity of Choosing Your Path Forward

The complexity of deciding to stay or leave after infidelity within a relationship is not understated; this choice carries immense weight for an individual's future happiness and overall well-being. Successful consideration demands introspection and uncovering your genuine needs and wants in a relationship while negotiating non-negotiables versus compromising. Engaging with your values will provide the foundation for making decisions that resonate with personal authenticity.

Deciding whether to mend or end requires thoughtfulness regarding all available options' impact on personal well-being - seek clarity to inform an informed choice. Choosing whether to stay or leave a relationship can be challenging. However, approach cautiously by following essential steps like gathering all available information, seeking adequate support, and evaluating the pros and cons of options while considering emotional growth opportunities and overall happiness within the connection.

External pressures from society can cloud our judgment in identifying our own needs and desires; hence it becomes critical not only breaking free from such expectations but also keeping personal well-being as a top priority while making crucial choices. Not letting social norms or others' opinions overshadow our intuition is essential, as what works best for us is more significant than meeting society's standards.

Trusting ourselves more than we rely on anything else while deciding about staying/leaving a relationship ensures moving forward with an informed mind rather than giving in to impulses/overwhelming emotions.

Empowering ourselves by prioritizing personal happiness and trusting our intuitive senses helps us make vital decisions in life. Our intuition often provides valuable wisdom when we face significant decisions concerning relationships. Tuning out external noise and tuning into our most profound feelings offers clues about what may be best for us in a given situation. Remember that prioritizing our well-being is critical when choosing partners who bring us genuine joy, fulfillment, and peace.

By employing practical tools like journaling or visualization exercises, we can create actionable healing plans or build new relationships with confidence in alignment with our core values. Deciding whether or not it's best for you and your well-being after facing infidelity can be arduous; weighing up options like staying put or taking off can leave one feeling overwhelmed at first glance- especially without adequate guidance.

This chapter seeks only but aims towards empowering you by equipping you with suitable tools necessary for tackling these challenges head-on while navigating through every step of the way. It's pertinent to recognize the importance and weight of this decision and understand that feelings of uncertainty, conflict, or downright confusion are entirely natural.

On the other hand, society has a way of putting expectations on people by pressuring them to stick around in relationships regardless of pain or betrayal. However, authentic empowerment comes from within by listening to our inner voice and prioritizing what we hold most dear- our happiness being one. Begin your journey towards self-discovery today: use self-reflection as a vital tool.

Take some time off for self-evaluation and understand what drives you, what motivates you, and what fulfills you. Deepen the knowledge aspect of it. What are the underlying convictions that guide your existence? What factors should remain etched in stone in any relationship? Streamlining these values will help evaluate seamlessly whether a bond resonates with long-term well-being. It's essential to rely on intuition which acts like a torchbearer illuminating obscure paths.

Please pay attention to those subtle suggestions, don't ignore them as they hold importance. Trust yourself, as nobody else understands what fits better for us than we do. Gathering all necessary information is crucial for informed choices. Objectively analyze various facets of the relationship - pros, cons, and prospects.

Make sure there has been a considerable improvement from the partner's side. Their efforts towards rebuilding trust align with our expectations. How devoted are they toward personal growth? Ask yourself if all these align with our needs and expectations.

Although seeking advice from close ones can be helpful during such times, remember that it's ultimately up to you when making decisions concerning your relationship after infidelity incidences occur.

Take caution against external influences or biases that could cloud proper judgment towards recovery/healing because everyone's journey is unique- What works for someone else won't always fit with another's lifestyle or needs.

Therefore: Trusting one's instincts about what suits them best when deciding on how they would wish their future relationships/paths would look like is essential – Such visualization factors into creating purposeful steps necessary for progress, whether rebuilding already-existing connections or starting anew- This does not mean any choice reflects poorly on someone's worth just because they had encountered infidelity.

This experience may challenge some, yet it does not define individuals entirely.

Everyone deserves to live a fulfilling life full of love, trust, and happiness: remembering one's innate strength, perseverance, and capability to decide and make choices that will serve the highest good is crucial.

The aftermath of infidelity can leave one feeling unsure about staying in an intimate relationship or not. Making such decisions requires careful consideration and self-awareness about personal values and priorities.

For an informed resolution aligned with overall well-being, this framework might help:

1 - Understand the weight of the final choice by acknowledging how detrimental it could be; give yourself room for emotional processing and obtain the necessary support from trusted family members/friends.

2 - Reflect deeply on personal values by drawing clarity on open compromise versus non-negotiable issues

3 - Evaluate current dynamics' strengths and weaknesses along with possible growth changes ahead

4 - Weigh the pros and cons of various possibilities regarding whether staying or leaving would deliver success in achieving desired results. Don't rush into any decisions when dealing with infidelity in relationships - take time to assess all available options carefully, considering yourself and those around you, such as children or other family members.

5 - In these situations, it can be tempting to seek advice from others but remember that ultimately the choice must come from within by trusting your instincts and listening to your gut feeling.

6 - After arriving at an informed decision, create an actionable plan for moving forward, such as seeking counseling or establishing healthy boundaries for future relationships should you decide on staying together.

Understand that everyone handles cheating differently, so don't compare yourself with others - focus instead on prioritizing your well-being.

We are eager to uncover all facets of infidelity recovery over the following chapters by providing helpful guides, knowledge, and concrete tools for your use along this road.

We will overcome these intricate barriers together through renewed introspection, re-identifying ourselves while shedding new light on personal growth opportunities constantly present throughout life's challenges.

You must have faith in yourself - believe that making healthy decisions is within reach for you! Take solace from this message: Hope will lead us toward a promising future full of happiness and newfound resilience.

Chapter 3: Unloving the Unfaithful: Rebuilding Trust and Self-Worth

Reclaiming Your Sense of Self Amidst Betrayal

Betrayal through infidelity can be detrimental when it comes down to relationships since it shatters their core foundations entirely - leaving one feeling lost and disconnected from their own identity and sense of worthiness.

To rebuild trust and rekindle their lost inner strength, one must begin by exploring their passions, interests, and values, which helps them reconnect with themselves beyond their inflicted pain. In many cases where individuals undergo stressors caused by cheating partners or similar instances find themselves experiencing deep wounds in their self-esteem - something they often struggle to acknowledge within themselves or dealing upfront.

But recovery begins by doing precisely that! Admitting these emotional scars within oneself makes the road to healing a reality.

It's pertinent to surround oneself with people who uplift and validate them through positive affirmations, self-talk, and activities that bring meaning to their lives. Undertaking therapy or counseling can provide a space where individuals may work through any lingering feelings of inadequacy or unworthiness that stem from infidelity.

By prioritizing and nurturing one's self-esteem, rebuilding their foundation of self-worth becomes achievable. When rebuilding trust after experiencing infidelity, focusing on self-care is crucial for promoting personal growth and emotional healing. Prioritizing practices that nurture the mind, body, and soul - such as mindfulness exercises or yoga - can help individuals cultivate inner peace and emotional resilience during a challenging time.

Additionally, taking care of physical health through regular exercise , nutrition , and rest ensures optimal wellness overall.

Setting healthy boundaries in relationships is equally important after betrayal has occurred.

Defining acceptable behavior sets expectations for partners regarding transparency , honesty, and respectfulness towards oneself. Communicating these boundaries firmly without compromise creates an environment conducive to healing while also preventing future occurrences of past hurts from happening again. Reinstating Confidence In One's Own Decision-Making And Self-Image:

The damage inflicted by infidelity extends beyond mistrust of one's partner, including self-doubt about one's judgment. To address this challenge, it is critical that an individual approach themselves with kindness and compassion while simultaneously forgiving a partner who has betrayed their trust.

It is essential to remember that someone else's actions do not define an individual nor detract from their ability to make sound choices; additionally, considering times when they have displayed skill or prior successes offers reassurance during times of uncertainty following a betrayal.

Establishing Guidelines To Support Progress In Rebuilding Trust Within A Relationship

Rebuilding lost trust within a relationship necessitates clarity surrounding rules and expectations between partners.

Regularly communicating about personal wants, concerns, and hopes makes it possible for both parties to collaborate on developing mutually agreeable boundaries that promote forgiveness and growth.

This process can involve cultivating transparency moving forward, improving communication skills, or engaging with couples therapy under the guidance of an experienced professional. Ultimately collective efforts at constructing healthy frameworks are vital in creating growth alongside resolutions.

Rebuilding trust after infidelity involves many challenges, but one crucial aspect is gaining back a healthy view of ourselves. My dear reader, Chapter 3 emphasizes how you can begin this process by reconnecting with your identity beyond the damage done by an unfaithful partner's actions.

Your sense of worthiness can be restored through compassionate reflection and self-care practices that support healing and growth combined with respectful boundary-setting within yourself and in future relationships.

At the same time, you navigate challenging times with strength. A healthy reminder amidst difficult times like those following infidelity: a person's value and worth are not determined by their partner's actions. It recommended that individuals take time to rediscover themselves by focusing on personal interests, passions, and skills that bring them joy.

Rebuilding one's self-esteem during such painful moments can significantly magnify the effects of this process. At first negative thoughts and feelings of inadequacy may seem impossible, but countering these beliefs with uplifting self-affirmations helps alleviate those doubts.

A supportive network surrounding oneself is fundamental in facilitating healing; engaging in nourishing activities like yoga or meditation further reinforces this support network. In addition to promoting relaxation techniques for mental health benefits, practicing self-care rituals can go hand in hand as an effective coping mechanism during recovery. If you're looking to prioritize your physical and emotional well-being after experiencing infidelity, there are a few key steps you can take.

First and foremost, ensure that you're taking care of your body through regular exercise, nutritious food, and adequate rest. Additionally, consider exploring therapeutic practices like journaling, art, or music to express your emotions and achieve greater clarity. Establishing healthy boundaries is critical to rebuilding trust in yourself and future relationships. These boundaries help protect your well-being while creating a framework for positive interactions with others.

To set effective boundaries, be sure to communicate them assertively and respectfully.

And don't be afraid to prioritize self-care without feeling guilty or hesitant.

Ultimately the journey toward rebuilding trust in yourself can be challenging after experiencing infidelity. But taking the time to reflect on past mistakes and growth can help cultivate self-compassion and forgiveness.

Remember that mistakes don't define you; you have the wisdom and discernment to make sound choices moving forward. Creating boundaries within the relationship can also foster healing and help rebuild trust over time.

By setting clear limits on what behaviors are acceptable (and aren't), both parties can move forward with greater confidence in each other's commitment to emotional health.

Healthy relationship boundaries are maintained through transparent communication between partners, voicing one's needs while being open-minded enough to consider those of their significant other sides.

Trust can only be rebuilt when genuine two-way respect exists; engaging in open dialogue is crucial for laying the groundwork of faith. It's vital to offer yourself kindness and patience to rediscover your self-worth.

HEALING MINDSET AFTER AN AFFAIR:

Coping with the aftermath of an affair is complex and challenging work for anyone involved - but there are ways to build resilience after this painful event to heal mentally over time.

The first step towards recovery is acknowledging the emotional response that often follows infidelity: sadness, shame, or anger, among many others, may arise within those experiencing this trauma.

By engaging these emotions head-on - speaking candidly with trusted friends or reaching out to mental health professionals - individuals can move towards processing these emotions in healthy ways instead of suppressing them.

Another crucial component towards building mental stamina revolves around prioritizing self-compassion over guilt trips as they work through their reactions; journaling experiences (as well as their goals and fears) or seeking out activities that feel healing can help individuals ground themselves in moments of stress or anxiety.

Finally, speaking openly with and listening to partners after an affair is crucial for building a stronger future. Gaining clarity on what happened, what everyone feels about it, and how to move forward can reassure all parties that they are working towards a productive solution rather than simply brushing the offense under the rug.

Rebuilding trust after infidelity requires honest communication that respects both parties involved without placing blame or making accusations.

It is common to feel a loss of confidence following an affair; however, by embarking on simple yet meaningful tasks, we can rebuild our self-worth – such as setting personal goals or exploring new passions.

If managing infidelity in your personal life proves too tricky, consider reaching out for professional support through therapy or counseling. Professional guidance with responses tailored precisely to your needs can go a long way during this difficult time.

Remember that overcoming infidelity takes time and deliberate effort- but doing so allows us the potential for greater emotional strength and happiness moving forward.

Although the healing process takes a great deal of courage and time, embracing the journey of self-discovery, nurturing inner strength, and recognizing inherent worthiness is essential. Keep taking forward steps in confidence, knowing that with each one comes discoveries about yourself that will strengthen your relationship in the future.

Chapter 4: When Words Are Empty: Signs of Genuine Remorse and Healing

Deciphering Empty Promises from Authentic Accountability

Following an instance of infidelity, it's crucial to differentiate authentic accountability from hollow reassurances. Words alone aren't enough to rebuild trust or heal from betrayal—consistent actions demonstrating legitimate remorse and a commitment to change are vital indicators.

Observe whether your partner takes responsibility for their actions, shows empathy towards your pain, and works actively on understanding and resolving any underlying issues leading up to their unfaithfulness. Remember: genuine remorse comes hand in hand with efforts towards repairing damaged relationships; those who take ownership of their mistakes will seek ways to make up for them while rebuilding bridges burned during moments of weakness.

In cases like this one, where pain runs deep following an affair, however, words will only go so far when it comes time for reconciliation because actions speak louder than those expressed promises, which may bring temporary solace but not resolution—pay close attention instead as our loved ones work to rebuild trust through substantial efforts such as increased transparency in communication or displaying a dedicated commitment towards personal growth and self-improvement.

To truly address the root causes of infidelity, we must genuinely heal ourselves while seeking lasting changes in our behaviors. One way to avoid disappointment after a betrayal is by being mindful of empty promises lacking substance or consistency from your partner. Communication plays a significant role in healing wounds caused by the breach of trust.

To achieve this, create an environment where you can safely share how you feel without holding back anything concerning your needs or concerns related to rebuilding trust. Expressing expectations about accountability is vital, and emphasizing genuine remorse is a non-negotiable factor in recovery.

It takes two people actively listening while expressing empathy when attempting open dialogue with one another for effective communication. An essential component of recovery is monitoring any consistent action resulting from growth on either side toward rebuilding trust.

Rebuilding trust after infidelity requires a mutual commitment from both partners toward taking responsibility for their actions and actively engaging in the healing process. Recognizing some critical indicators of genuine remorse remains essential when navigating this challenging journey together.

Examples include heartfelt apologies devoid of excuses or justifications; consistent efforts to rebuild trust by demonstrating work on making amends; openness towards seeking forgiveness while acknowledging how hurtful their behavior was; having empathy towards the hurt they've caused.

When healing from infidelity, it's essential to recognize that effort requires equal participation from both partners - open communication, empathy, and a genuine willingness to change can go a long way in creating mutual support systems between each other. By establishing shared responsibility at the outset, you can navigate these complexities together while recognizing accountability as paramount.

Authentic remorse must be present rather than empty promises when building trust as they signal genuine commitment towards growth. Ensure clear communication between both parties by creating an environment where candid discussions about experiences can occur without judgment or retribution.

Evaluate your partner's behavioral changes - have they genuinely committed to understanding or just going through superficial motions? Highlight key indicators suggestive thereof, such as utterances demonstrating sincere remorse without excuses or justifications.

Encourage shared responsibility by encouraging each other's active participation in rebuilding this damaged relationship through mutual forgiveness; at times, recognizing past mistakes may have led us here, but now looking forward to new growth potential together. As you work towards healing after experiencing infidelity in your relationship, it's essential to remember that actions carry more weight than words alone.

For trust to be rebuilt, you must search for genuine regret from your partner - accompanied by an earnest desire for transformation and tangible behaviors demonstrating their promise towards such change.

Establishing honesty-driven communication channels with your partner is one way of navigating this journey toward rebuilding relational healthiness.

Chapter 4 in this guide tackles an essential topic: discerning between empty promises versus authentic expressions of guilt and a pledge towards personal growth following infidelity betrayal. Mere commitment without corresponding tangible changes may not suffice in mending broken relationships - hence this chapter equips individuals with tools enabling dependable differentiation between such scenarios as they aim at reconnecting positively amid the turmoil.

Identifying signs of genuine remorse and commitment to change is one critical step toward post-infidelity recovery.

Your partner's consistent growth and positive transformations are essential in determining progress toward restoring relational trustworthiness after infidelity. While acknowledging the hurt caused may be a sign of remorse, comprehending the underlying factors that caused the betrayal and an authentic promise towards self-growth and positive changes marks hopeful progress.

Navigating the recovery process following infidelity requires close attention to several key factors within your partner, such as humility, empathy, and honesty about their desire to make positive changes in the relationship moving forward. Trekking down the road of recovery requires more than mere words; consistent action over time is a crucial piece of the puzzle.

Building back trust requires transparency and vulnerability between both partners, as they must engage in meaningful conversations about their feelings regarding what has occurred. Finding ways to communicate effectively is paramount, and this chapter provides practical guidance on how best to do so while keeping respect front and center during these interactions.

Recognizing a person's level of remorse and commitment focuses on ongoing efforts such as taking accountability and attending counseling or therapy sessions consistently alongside displaying efforts that aim at rebuilding shattered levels of trust, indicating an unwavering intent moving forward.

Changing one's ways authentically entails addressing unhealthy patterns head-on while seeking expert assistance.

An enduring commitment towards continuous personal growth and self-improvement is also mandatory to heal relationships genuinely impacted by infidelity. Inculcating open dialogues between partners and shared accountability paramountly marks this chapter's essence.

Creating a safe atmosphere where each partner can articulate their needs without fear fosters mutual vulnerability that instills empathy and understanding in both individuals - vital ingredients for rebuilding trust and promoting unity again in such situations like these- where cheating has caused ruptures between two people involved emotionally or otherwise closely linked with each other.

Active involvement from both partners in reparation efforts helps spread out the onus evenly, leading to solidifying trust and commitment, outlined further in Chapter 5 (next part).

Accessing valuable insights via trained professionals such as therapists or counselors becomes essential for navigating complexities in reconceptualizing the relationship.

Together, these chapters form a holistic guide that enlightens readers with knowledge of theoretical and practical tools accompanied by peerless emotional support crucial to healing, growing, and rebuilding after infidelity.

Chapter 5: Counseling as a Lifeline: Reconnecting and Communicating After Infidelity

The Transformative Power of Professional Guidance

Infidelity can be incredibly damaging to any relationship - upending trust and intimacy while leaving couples feeling lost and unmoored from one another.

However, seeking professional help during this challenging time can provide hope and guidance toward healing and restoring the bond between partners. Here are some reasons why counseling could be precisely what you need during infidelity recovery:

Counseling offers a safe place for couples who may feel disconnected or unable to communicate effectively with one another following an affair.

Without fearing judgment or shame, a counselor helps couples navigate their emotions providing valuable insights that drive transformational change throughout the recovery journey.

Choosing the right therapist is crucial when seeking support after an affair in your relationship - but not all therapists specialize in relationships or have experience in infidelity recovery. You may consider different therapeutic approaches, including Cognitive Behavioral Therapy, Emotionally Focused Therapy, and the Gottman Method of Couples Therapy.

Understanding the benefits of each system can help you choose the type of therapy that best suits your unique needs.

Lastly, successful counseling requires active participation from both parties involved - including honest self-reflection, active listening, and a commitment to vulnerability. Couples can significantly enhance their chances of healing and rebuilding together by engaging with their therapist openly and honestly during sessions.

Acquiring Deeper Self-Insights Through Counseling:

Attending counseling sessions can provide valuable insights into one's emotions, motivations, and patterns of interaction.

By engaging in active participation during these sessions, couples can successfully acquire the necessary tools to rebuild their relationship after an instance of infidelity. Effective communication is essential in rebuilding trust and intimacy following an affair.

One way to achieve this is by enhancing communication skills through strategies that cultivate understanding and empathy. Active listening and validating each other's experiences while practicing compassion are essential techniques that enable individuals to express their needs constructively – forming the foundation for open conversations.

Rebuilding emotional or physical intimacy after an affair can be challenging; however, it is not impossible, primarily when both parties work intentionally towards fostering open dialogues that encourage vulnerability within the relationship.

This chapter outlines techniques couples can use to regain mutual trust while strengthening emotional bonds. It takes more than just practical approaches to mend an emotional connection damaged by infidelity, as discussed in Chapter 5.

Apart from engaging in shared activities or exploring sensual experiences with your partner, it also requires seeking professional guidance through counseling sessions.

A qualified therapist or counselor provides essential support through insights into navigating complexities when rebuilding trust and fostering effective communication. Recovery from the pain caused by infidelity often requires professional help - this chapter delves into why seeking assistance from therapists/counselors is beneficial for many reasons.

The emotional complexity of an affair makes it challenging to manage without expert guidance; having an experienced person by your side can offer validation and much-needed support while helping you navigate complex feelings.

Understanding the implications of infidelity on relationships requires specialized expertise in therapy; exploring underlying problems takes skill, too - both factors make finding the right therapist/counselor essential for success in overcoming this difficult time.

To assist in selecting an appropriate professional, this chapter guides readers through some considerations, including experience in recovery from infidelity situations, preferred therapeutic approach, and capability of creating safe and supportive environments.

By working with someone who values similar things as yourself- establishing a solid therapeutic alliance becomes achievable so that individuals may feel empowered on their journey toward healing. To make an informed decision about which type of therapy best suits your needs and goals, it's crucial to understand the various approaches available.

Actively participating in counseling sessions maximizes therapeutic benefits for individuals seeking help. This chapter emphasizes the importance of engaging in therapeutic processes by being open-minded towards self-reflection techniques offered throughout sessions while applying strategies discussed altogether.

HEALING POWER OF GRATITUDE AFTER THE BETRAYAL:

Healing wounds resulting from betrayal often presents itself as an intricate process one must navigate sensitively. Nonetheless, focusing on practical techniques such as harnessing the power of gratitude can offer immense aid when building a resilient spirit post-betrayal.

Gratitude involves recognizing and expressing an appreciation for the good things in life, even during unpleasant experiences.

Several studies have identified that fostering gratitude can yield positive aspects such as happy thoughts, reduced stress levels, and enhanced interpersonal bonds.

Cultivating a grateful outlook after betrayal can establish a positive foundation for moving forward. To do this practically, individuals can incorporate practices such as daily recording three to five things they're grateful for through journaling or mental reflection. Focusing on the good things in life can help shift our overall mindset towards positivity and ignite feelings of gratitude.

Incorporating gratitude into meditation is an effective tool for cultivating mindfulness and reducing stress. By focusing on things that inspire feelings of gratefulness, such as people or experiences, one can foster an appreciation for present moments.

One way to actively create opportunities for appreciating life's blessings is by engaging in acts of kindness towards others. Volunteering time or resources toward charitable causes or simply being kinder towards loved ones are ways that individuals can start shifting their perspective towards gratitude.

Putting pen to paper by writing a letter expressing appreciation is another proven method for developing feelings of positivity and thankfulness. The power of expressing thanks can't be overstated when it comes to strengthening relationships and cultivating positivity in your life.

A straightforward yet impactful method is by writing a letter expressing gratitude towards someone who positively impacted or influenced you on an individual level. Share specific details about how their support has contributed positively to various aspects of your life and their importance. The road to healing after experiencing betrayal can be rocky and grueling, but incorporating gratitude into our daily routine proves beneficial.

This could mean setting designated moments each day for expressing appreciation or engaging in other rituals like lighting candles or offering prayers of thanksgiving. These activities instill in us a sense of gratefulness for all the good things happening around us and encourage us to make positive impacts wherever possible.

Cultivating an attitude of gratitude is crucial when recovering from betrayal; it helps shift our mindset towards positivity and provides practical ways for moving forward by harnessing its therapeutic benefits through various activities like meditation, random acts of kindness, walking for mindfulness, or writing letters expressing our thankfulness.

Therapy provides an opportunity for personal growth and transformation; thus, investing oneself entirely in it facilitates profound healing with positive results effectively accomplished as Chapter 5 concludes setting up future chapters well-prepared for communication skills building as they remain essential throughout relationships, life-spans on various levels -- from workmates or family members alike!

Together these chapters create a comprehensive guide empowering people who wish to navigate infidelity recovery challenges while re-establishing emotional bonds yet creating fulfilling, resilient ones.

Chapter 6: The Breaking Point: Recognizing When Efforts No Longer Suffice

Navigating the Threshold of Exhaustion and Self-Care:

Recovering from infidelity is challenging and can leave us emotionally and physically drained. It's essential to recognize the warning signs of exhaustion early on so that we can prioritize self-care as a necessary part of restoring our strength and clarity. This chapter offers guidance on navigating through this challenging time while safeguarding your overall sense of wellness.

Infidelity recovery can be a taxing experience that often leads to chronic fatigue, irritability, lack of motivation, and increased stress levels. By staying vigilant against these warning signs, we're better equipped to take measures designed to counteract exhaustion before it deepens.

Implementing self-care practices tailored to your unique needs is another crucial aspect of recovering from infidelity successfully. This may involve engaging in activities that bring you joy or fulfillment (such as hobbies), seeking support from trusted loved ones when you need it most (or professional counseling), or dedicating time to improving your physical health.

Lastly, establishing healthy boundaries with those around you is vital for safeguarding emotional well-being during this time.

Edges allow space away from toxic relationships while allowing room for self-care and personal growth. Maintaining control and avoiding additional harm necessitates establishing well-defined boundaries within a relationship. This segment offers insight into best practices for boundary setting while highlighting effective communication techniques.

Rebuilding a partnership following infidelity necessitates considerable effort and commitment; nevertheless, there may be a moment when those exertions produce diminishing returns.

In this chapter, we'll examine how recognizing one's limitations can prove beneficial by enabling individuals to reevaluate the direction of their partnership. As we approach Chapter 6, it's time to face one of the most challenging aspects of post-infidelity recovery: recognizing when our attempts at repairing damaged relationships have reached their limit.

To move forward effectively in this process, practicing honest self-assessment is crucial as we evaluate whether remaining in the relationship truly serves each partner's well-being. The chapter guides us through reevaluating our needs while considering alternative routes once all avenues toward reconciliation have been exhausted.

This section offers support for exploring new possibilities by seeking professional advice if necessary so that informed choices regarding future relationships can be made confidently.

To safeguard against emotional burnout during this challenging period, it's essential to recognize signs of exhaustion proactively while prioritizing effective self-care techniques—setting boundaries where appropriate while acknowledging personal limits—also ensures continued health and well-being throughout the recovery stage.

Chapter 6 provides readers with clear guidance on navigating post-infidelity endpoints successfully and offers an essential roadmap for anyone struggling to make well-informed decisions that align with personal needs and goals. Despite one's best intentions, infidelity can lead to irreversible damage within a relationship.

At times like these staying in the partnership may not benefit an individual's overall well-being anymore. In this chapter, readers are urged to become more self-aware by recognizing signs of emotional and physical exhaustion as they arise. Infidelity affects both partners involved deeply, so upholding personal boundaries is necessary at breaking points within relationships. Recognizing where one stands empowers individuals to prioritize their happiness while guarding against further harm.

This chapter also emphasizes the importance of setting healthy boundaries while highlighting how crucial building solid support systems is for gaining emotional strength during tough times.

Honest reflection becomes paramount when considering whether rebuilding efforts within a relationship is no longer sufficient.

Chapter 6 provides readers with guidance on evaluating post-infidelity progress per their expectations and needs. Deciding to leave a relationship following infidelity is an arduous process that should be approached with self-assurance in one's intuition and judgment.

To gain clarity in this decision-making process seeking support from professionals specializing in therapy or counseling can provide valuable assistance. It is essential to reevaluate personal needs when considering alternative paths toward moving forward.

Letting go of third-party connections related to infidelity marks a crucial step towards healing oneself, clearing space for growth towards new beginnings, discussed further in the next chapter on establishing boundaries while minimizing external influences detrimental to progress.

It must be noted that recognizing when attempts at mending relationships no longer serve one's well-being do not equate to failure but instead takes strength and courage towards establishing clear-cut boundaries according to personal needs - all serving as a means towards opening oneself up towards greater happiness.

WHEN I'M SURE THAT I WANT A DIVORCE:

Divorce ranks among life's most significant events requiring careful self-reflection before taking drastic measures. Emotions may run high, but there are ways for couples to contemplate this daunting step to determine if it's necessary at all.

Journaling one's feelings provides an opportunity for introspection and clarity, while engaging with professional counselors helps wade through the complexities arising from such difficult decisions.

If still unsure, it's advisable to consider the long-term effects of going down this path - how will it shape your financial future? Will you be emotionally and mentally prepared to navigate life after that?

Contextualizing divorce regarding values and goals is critical in making informed decisions. Divorce isn't a decision to take lightly. Numerous factors are involved, including finance, familial obligations, and safety nets like social support systems which must be considered before taking action.

Patterns within relationships can also provide valuable information regarding underlying conflicts or dissatisfaction within partnerships; if these situations regularly appear in yours, then perhaps it's time to consider separating from one another when deciding on divorce.

Trusting your instincts and listening to what feels suitable for you and your life is vital. Don't hesitate to seek professional assistance for further guidance or support.

The weighty nature of divorce calls for thoughtful consideration. Yet it can also give rise to new beginnings by enabling individuals to build happier and healthier lives.

My academic pursuits at university have instilled a propensity toward investigation and scholarly composition.

Therefore, producing cogent prose necessitates an unwavering dedication to transparency and coherence.

Language mechanics such as correct grammar usage and syntactical accuracy are indispensable components of effective communication, as testified by celebrated wordsmith Stephen King who declared that "the adverb is not your friend."

Chapter 7: Severing Ties: Letting Go of Third-Party Connections for Good

Understanding the Impact of Continued Contact on Healing:

When healing from infidelity, recognizing how third-party connections impact recovery is critical. This chapter delves into the intricacies of managing relationships with those involved in adultery and offers practical advice on creating boundaries and minimizing external influences.

Third-party relationships like a lover or mutual friends who knew about the affair can significantly impact progress towards healing.

Understanding how these individuals may hinder progress is essential, and whether cutting ties is necessary to facilitate recovery is critical. However, severing connections can be emotionally challenging and complex.

This section guides various scenarios that may arise to help navigate this process while prioritizing one's well-being to create a clear path toward healing. Infidelity can have catastrophic impacts on one's life; therefore, establishing clear boundaries becomes essential in safeguarding oneself and promoting healing.

This chapter offers practical advice on how to set such parameters with individuals who may have been involved or have knowledge about the incident; this helps reduce external triggers that could impede progress or trigger negative emotions.

The closure is paramount when attempting to move forward after betrayal. Letting go of toxic relationships becomes inevitable in achieving this resolution and acceptance; hence this section highlights different strategies for attaining closure- honest communication, professional help-seeking, or personal rituals, among others- each geared towards promoting resolution and acceptance that are fundamental components of any healing journey.

By releasing emotional baggage through finding closure, one creates ample room for new opportunities that may arise from within their healing process- a chance to critically explore what life has to offer post-infidelity experience.

In light of this reality letting go of unhealthy attachments becomes crucial even though it comes with its challenges; nevertheless, it remains an essential step towards a healthier future.

Creating distance from individuals causing us harm is necessary if we want to heal from their impact on our lives.

Chapter 7 presents practical strategies for detaching ourselves emotionally from third-party connections involved in infidelity that have had such an effect on us. These include setting boundaries, practicing self-care, and prioritizing growth and well-being.

Moreover, we stress how important it is to have supportive people around us during this time, like trusted friends or family members who will guide us as we sever these ties. Moving forward after infidelity requires careful consideration of how external influences impact the healing process. It's essential to effectively cut ties with third-party connections and guides, creating boundaries that facilitate proper healing.

Severing such ties may evoke emotions like guilt or attachment, hindering recovery. This guide addresses these emotional challenges by providing practical strategies for gradual distancing rather than sudden detachment.

This approach safeguards your emotional well-being while allowing you to create space for new and healthier relationships to flourish.

By implementing such strategies, you'll reclaim your sense of self and rebuild trust slowly but steadily - all while moving forward positively toward a brighter future.

By severing ties with external links, you unlock the potential for personal growth, discovering yourself more fully while laying the groundwork for a happier future. Chapter 7 serves as a bridge leading into the next chapter, which focuses on evaluating progress in one's relationship.

Rebuilding trust after infidelity can be rife with hills and valleys, making recognizing signs of growth or stagnation crucial. The following chapter provides vital tools to assess one's headway while cultivating an evolving bond built upon mutual commitment.

Relinquishing ties takes boldness - an action born out of self-care and respect towards oneself - creating space for healing while minimizing external influences by setting boundaries to prioritize our well-being so we can reclaim our narrative on how we live life.

On this path, know that you walk alongside others, seeking your renewed hopefulness, authenticity, and fulfillment.

The presence of micromanagement within the workplace environment has been observed by professionals with higher education qualifications as potentially counterproductive.

Examples include over-monitoring or redundant administrative demands placed on staff members, reducing morale and lowering productivity outcomes.

While research has shown that high levels of management control are associated with elevated stress levels among workers, this also increases the chance of them leaving their current employment situation at a greater rate than those who enjoy more flexibility from management direction.

Therefore managers would be wise to promote their team's independent action and trust their ability to call on constructive input only when necessary.

ENDING ALL CONTACT:

Ending all contact with an unfaithful spouse is never easy but sometimes necessary to move forward more healthily. Here are some tips that may help:

Firstly, communicate clearly and directly when stating your intentions about cutting off all communication. This clarity will allow both parties to understand what's at stake and make the necessary adjustments moving forward.

Secondly, block their phone number on all devices promptly after separation to avoid any triggers or unnecessary reminders of the past. Social media channels should also be blocked from their end ASAP - this includes Facebook, Twitter, etc...

Lastly - change passwords immediately on shared accounts such as banking or emails. This action protects both parties from potential fraud down the line.

Following these steps, you can safeguard your emotional well-being while ensuring they have no unwanted access from now on - helping promote healing for both sides. Parting ways with an ex-partner can trigger emotional distress but don't forget to always focus on safety. Safeguarding personal information and accounts by changing passwords and security settings puts oneself first when protecting against intrusion from the former spouse.

It's also essential to consider temporarily disconnecting oneself from mutual contacts such as friends or family members who may mediate contact attempts. These measures are necessary to ensure a peaceful process of healing. When coping with negative emotions like guilt or loneliness, reaching out for emotional support from reliable sources such as friends or mental health professionals becomes essential. Remember - prioritizing individual emotional well-being is vital to achieving rehabilitation post-breakup.

IF YOU WORK WITH THE AFFAIR PARTNER:

Working alongside an affair partner can be uncomfortable, but setting proper boundaries is vital to maintain professionalism while protecting your marriage's sanctity.

1 - To this end, ensure that there are no personal conversations shared between both parties but rather solely focused on necessary discussions regarding work matters only while maintaining distance physically.

2 - Treating the affair partner as any other colleague also helps reduce workplace tensions since it eliminates any notion that favorable treatment is being provided. Avoiding flirtatious or inappropriate behaviors that could cause misunderstandings should be a priority to ensure that the working relationship stays strictly professional.

3 - Minimizing communication will positively impact all parties and prevent unnecessary risks. Use email or instant messaging platforms

as alternatives when necessary while avoiding phone calls or text messages that do not relate to work matters.

4 - Avoiding other emotional attachments or inappropriate behavior resulting from your affair calls for limited communication between yourself and that partner.

5 - Additionally, minimize alone time together wherever possible, especially if work-related stuff or meetings require privacy - choose public places/well-lit rooms instead.

6 - In situations where privacy is crucial, have an open-door policy or have someone else present in the room apart from just the two of you. Being truthful and communicating openly with your spouse about how hard you're actively working towards avoiding unfavorable situations between yourself and your affair partner can help rebuild trust and reinforce marital commitment.

7 - Coping mechanisms like seeking support from trusted family/friends/qualified therapists can be valuable during emotionally draining times. Getting an outsider's perspective and emotional support can be beneficial during a tough time.

You can use the following practical tips to handle the affair partner while safeguarding yourself and your non-guilty spouse. Honesty is crucial, and prioritizing your commitment to your marriage should remain paramount.

Chapter 8: The Stagnant Journey: Assessing Progress in the Relationship

Evaluating the Signs of Growth or Stagnation in Post-Infidelity Recovery

Working through infidelity in a relationship requires ongoing effort by both partners involved. This chapter offers practical advice for couples engaging in post-infidelity recovery by examining signs of progress indicating positive partnership changes.

Improvements like better communication between partners and increased mutual trust are key factors that signal growth within one post-infidelity journey together.

However, obstacles may surface during this time - recurring negative patterns from past behaviors or difficulties addressing lingering emotional wounds from hurtful actions.

To help couples navigate these challenges effectively, this chapter offers insight into fostering effective communication and seeking professional help.

To recover from infidelity, effective communication is critical. Our section provides practical advice for fostering constructive conversations between partners through active listening, constructive expression of emotions, empathy building, and conflict resolution techniques that benefit all parties involved.

Post-infidelity recovery demands change and growth to rebuild your relationship effectively. This chapter urges couples to prioritize personal development to create an environment conducive to dynamic growth over time, leading towards nurturing a robust and resilient bond.

Rebuilding trust after infidelity necessitates both partners taking joint responsibility by committing themselves fully while actively participating in the healing process through consistent actions that foster trust rebuilding, where everyone takes full ownership of their role in the relationship.

Moving forward from infidelity requires immense support from one's partner and oneself. Building accountability helps reinforce commitment when rebuilding trust, which starts by creating a nonjudgmental space where both individuals can share vulnerabilities freely while promoting empathy for one another, leading to more significant emotional connections and enabling further growth into a long-term successful relationship full of happiness despite past adversities.

This chapter also suggests periodically assessing progress by identifying hurdles as soon as they arise and using effective communication to allow continued progress. Evaluating your progress after infidelity, identifying potential roadblocks, and nurturing a healthy relationship built on mutual commitment are imperative.

Rebuilding trust after cheating isn't always straightforward; evaluating where you stand is essential to move forward.

This chapter encourages introspection by providing tools for recognizing personal growth and collective advancement within the partnership- like better communication skills or increased empathy towards one another -that signify progress in rebuilding trust.

But it's also crucial to tackle obstacles that might get in the way of this possible success story- think lingering resentment or unresolved emotions between partners- which this chapter examines closely with practical solutions to overcome them effectively.

The central theme of Chapter 8 revolves around cultivating a dynamic partnership based on mutual commitment- embracing changes along the way while prioritizing growth together.

When rebuilding trust after broken bonds have occurred within a relationship, it's essential to remember that this journey doesn't have a set end point; there will always be opportunities for growth going forward when both parties remain committed to improvement together over time.

Finding a balance between commitments is crucial when healing your relationship from past hurtfulness or wrongdoing. Taking an active role toward equal participation can foster an environment of understanding and healthy communication so that real progress can be assessed.

Though there may be setbacks, each milestone should be celebrated as a reminder of how far you've come in this ongoing journey to rebuild trust together. With patience and effort, a stronger foundation of mutual growth can take place – preparing you and your partner for the upcoming chapter, where different strategies focused on enhancing commitment will be explored.

Step by step, you're constructing a life overflowing with affection, comprehension, and relationships. Continue on this path and watch as your future blossoms into something beautiful.

PRACTICAL EXAMPLES OF EXERCISES AND ACTIVITIES FOR ASSESSING PROGRESS IN POST-INFIDELITY RECOVERY:

Establishing regular progress evaluation schedules and pinpointing areas that require improvement are essential in a post-infidelity recovery plan. Below are some practical exercises and activities couples can undertake to assess their growth:

Reflection Time: Schedule reflection time on a routine basis, where both parties of the relationship can discuss progress made since the initial infidelity event occurred. Consider improvements achieved, challenges faced and successfully overcome, and future goals.

Communication Exercises: Promote active listening and non-judgmental communication within your relationship. An effective exercise is taking uninterrupted turns and sharing thoughts and feelings- this promotes understanding.

Love-Language Assessment- Assess what specific love language each partner prefers; this way, couples understand how to communicate affection effectively. Teams must prioritize building trust through meaningful activities that foster teamwork or sharing personal information to overcome stagnation during post-infidelity recovery. This increases bonding and trust levels between both partners.

However, if the growth seems stalled despite these efforts, certain alternative practices may be beneficial. Seeking out couples therapy with an infidelity recovery specialist offers unparalleled guidance and support while helping both parties work through any lingering issues.

In addition to this therapeutic approach, self-care practices such as individualized therapy sessions, meditation exercises, or consistent exercise routines offer opportunities for personal growth amidst stress.

A couple's retreat can also provide a substantial perspective shift for those seeking broader insight into their relationship as they move forward together after infidelity has occurred. Couples seeking support while working through tough times have various options. Retreats present a haven whereby both partners can focus on finding solutions together while building bonds that'll enable them to weather any storms thrown their way. Should one desire more guidance on navigating such delicate situations or improving upon foundational aspects of one's dynamic with their partner, seminars are an excellent resource available for the same. With numerous activities designed around fostering growth in relationships alongside coping mechanisms aimed at surmounting difficulties such as infidelity, all parties concerned will benefit from actively engaging with each other during these events.

Rebuilding trust after such a betrayal is no easy feat. However, practicing exercises to keep track of progress made will aid in maintaining momentum toward achieving a more robust, healthier relationship.

Chapter 9: Unbalanced Commitment: Sharing the Burden of Rebuilding

Recognizing the Importance of Equal Effort in Healing

If you're trying to repair your relationship after infidelity, it'll take dedication from both partners. This chapter explores why finding balance in that commitment is vital to success.

I also share signs indicating one person may not be doing their fair share. I offer suggestions for ensuring mutual commitment and participation throughout your healing journey; open communication is essential for a relationship to heal after infidelity.

Promoting transparency through honest conversations, active listening techniques, constructively expressing emotions, and practicing empathy are essential. A safe and trusting environment is created for both partners to heal in unison by fostering open communication.

We are exploring the idea that rebuilding trust after infidelity requires a joint effort from both partners. It emphasizes the significance of mutual commitment and equal dedication toward the recovery journey.

We must focus on how shared responsibility helps establish strong trust and accountability between partners. Celebrating essential milestones together is also vital in strengthening their bond even further.

Recognizing the importance of active engagement from both parties is essential when rebuilding trust after infidelity.

This means putting in equal amounts of effort identifying areas where there may be signs of inequality and taking practical steps towards healing.

The significance of balanced commitment between both partners during their journey towards recovery post-infidelity, where uneven efforts could have negative consequences on mutual healing prospects, hence highlighting several strategies for fostering mutual commitment alongside active participation, such as building a solid foundation based on trust plus accountability which aids in the promotion of growth for the relationship devoid of any biases, is fundamental also explores practical techniques centered around transparency, open communication, shared responsibility and setting healthy boundaries- while also detailing strategies for maintaining consistency between actions and intentions which is paramount in gaining back trustworthiness.

I want to conclude this chapter by presenting the delicate balance between managing conflicts while ensuring that children are protected, where prioritizing their well-being remains a top priority, ultimately reminding us that rebuilding trust requires active investment from both partners through empathy, mutual support, and open dialogue.

Creating a solid foundation based on equal levels of devotion is critical if you want to strengthen your relationship over time. The upcoming section will examine some difficulties in protecting innocence while navigating tension-filled situations involving children or family members.

You'll get step-by-step instructions on fostering an encouraging environment for kids while co-parenting with ease alongside your partner - understanding how separation might serve everyone's best interests when necessary.

On this journey toward transformational change together, remember that shared commitment coupled with an aim towards mutual growth remain core components required if we hope to rebuild trust and create a promising future for ourselves, our partner, and all the children involved.

PROMOTING TRANSPARENCY:

Re-establishing trust after experiencing infidelity necessitates promoting transparency and open lines of communication between partners - both critical components of rebuilding any relationship's foundation.

Though every couple's situation may differ slightly from one another based on their unique circumstances yet, here are pragmatic recommendations that could enable more honest conversations:

It is necessary first to dedicate quality time devoid of distractions strictly for communicating with your partner if you're seeking openness and transparency in your relationship following infidelity incidents.

Furthermore, when dealing with complex subjects during these interactions with your spouse/loved one has sincerity when expressing yourselves instead of watering down anything difficult or uncomfortable; thereby avoiding misunderstandings or uncertain situations that could endanger building trust afresh among couples.

Additionally, active listening is pivotal in effective communication, demonstrating that you put effort into comprehending your partner's message, making them feel heard, and boosting their trust in you.

Openness is the key to fostering trust and creating a transparent relationship with your significant other. It's essential to share information about your daily activities and convey thoughts and feelings honestly without hesitation. This may entail disclosing social media account passwords or email addresses.

Using technology can help promote transparency between partners; GPS tracking or phone usage tracker apps could help monitor each other's whereabouts if used respectfully without invading one another's privacy.

If communication issues impede progress within the relationship seeking counseling services from professionals offers immense benefits when developing healthy communication habits thoughtfully over time.

Rebuilding trust takes earnest effort and patience from both parties involved; working together towards transparency by taking small steps would eventually lead to better results than expecting instant change overnight.

Promoting transparency while ensuring open communication is an intricate process that necessitates unwavering determination from both couple members.

Nevertheless, these practical tips can go a long way towards developing trust and solidifying your bond with one another over the years.

Chapter 10: Protecting Innocence: Children, Conflict, and the Decision to Leave

Navigating the Challenging Terrain of Parenthood and Separation

Infidelity not only shakes up romantic relationships; it also affects children and parenting dynamics. Our focus in this chapter is on examining how infidelity impacts kids offering practical tips on protecting them from conflict and weighing up whether leaving the relationship is worth considering since it could affect them profoundly.

An affair creates a ripple effect that has far-reaching consequences, even for young family members. Here we delve into how infidelity affects kids emotionally and psychologically while emphasizing the importance of safeguarding their well-being amid all the upheaval. We also guide managing their emotions should they react negatively.

Shielding your kids from disputes or tensions sparked by infidelity is critical; this chapter provides hands-on advice on maintaining healthy family dynamics despite everything around you.

I recommend minimizing arguments around your kids as much as possible while ensuring you retain consistent routines that offer reassurance when they need it most. Here at our program, one central area we explore involves showing people strategies for communicating more effectively and resolving conflicts more productively in relationships, particularly when things get challenging over time.

However, things can get even more complex when deciding about troubled partnerships where children are involved.

I want to help you work through these challenging issues by providing guidance on weighing the potential impact of your relationship choices on your children.

By thinking through crucial factors like how well you can co-parent together and just how much conflict there is, you'll be better equipped to make a choice that prioritizes the well-being of your kids.

Separation might become an option necessary for everyone's well-being. If staying in a troubled relationship poses more harm than benefit, this section guides recognizing these signs, such as chronic conflict or a toxic atmosphere that negatively affects everyone involved.

As parents navigate infidelity challenges with their children providing ample support and resources fosters open communication by creating a safe space where children can express themselves without fear of judgment. Professional help remains accessible if needed to ensure proper healing and successful post-trauma adjustment.

Caring for your child means always prioritizing their well-being amidst any challenges brought about by situations such as infidelity—this calls for careful navigation by shielding them from potential conflicts at home while also evaluating whether separation could be the best course of action with the help of professional advice.

Always prioritize your kids' well-being when making choices or taking action.

Protecting Innocence: Children, Conflict, and the Decision to Leave

This chapter covers the complex realm of parenthood versus infidelity's effects on offspring. This chapter recognizes the challenges of balancing conflict management with putting one's children first while deciding if a relationship is worth continuing.

It's essential to create an environment that fosters support for one another as co-parents while navigating these circumstances effectively.

A crucial aspect is safeguarding their childhood innocence in light of infidelity after-effects; understanding how conflict can affect them emotionally is essential because it impacts their mental health long-term positively/negatively based upon circumstance severity-at-hand such as betrayal trauma syndrome -BTS- (Freyd et al., 2008).

Offering techniques for creating a healthy atmosphere alleviates adverse outcomes while promoting their emotional health through empathy-based restoration (Gottman and Levenson, 2000).

As a parent, it is imperative to keep their best interests at the forefront while considering what's next for the family. I bring you valuable resources for effective co-parenting strategies, promoting open communication channels and cooperative approaches even during tough times.

Undoubtedly, children's well-being should be the top priority despite the personal pains or uncertainties parents may face.

One crucial step towards informed decision-making is acknowledging how relationship dynamics can affect kids drastically.

We have discussed practical insights to assess whether staying in an unhealthy relationship is worth it or when separation becomes necessary for all involved parties' betterment.

Furthermore, it guides parents in navigating complexities around co-parenting practices while ensuring a stable and nurturing environment for their kids amidst ongoing conflicts.

As Chapter 10 concludes with these critical aspects of parenting explored comprehensively, Chapter 11 will take you through rebuilding physical intimacy after infidelity and betrayals between partners.

It exposes emotional complexities and fears involved in fostering trust and vulnerability as critical pillars of rebuilding confidence in each other to rekindle closeness again.

Keeping children innocent and secure is everybody's responsibility.

It is a valuable lesson to co-parenting effectively, nourishing an encouraging home atmosphere while prioritizing our young one's emotions as we make life-changing decisions amidst strife.

It is vital to remember that during parental challenges with conflict situations never lose sight of offering our cherished ones an unreservedly calm ambiance coupled with the utmost protection available from us parents or guardians alike.

PROTECTING INNOCENCE:

Helping children through the healing and adjustment phase after separation can evoke many emotions and challenges. It's paramount to note that every child goes about this phase differently based on age, personality traits, and circumstances surrounding the separation. To help navigate through this process more effectively, this section aims to provide practical guidance.

Encourage Open Communication: Honesty in communication is critical during these times; allow them space to communicate their thoughts freely without fear of judgment or criticism. Avoid speaking negatively about your ex-partner around your kids, as it might affect them emotionally.

Instead, facilitate creative ways they can express themselves, such as art therapy, writing stories, and playing games that could prove therapeutic in due time.

Maintain a Stable Routine: Children find comfort in consistent and structured environments; keeping regular schedules for meals, bedtime, and other activities as much as possible can provide stability amidst all the chaos and uncertainty associated with separation.

During divorce/separation, children tend to have questions and deep-seated concerns that require deliberate attention from the parties involved.

Addressing these queries transparently- taking care not to overburden the child- by reassuring them of their safety while empathizing with them remains important throughout this transition period.

Ensure that your child has access to a supportive environment where they can still interact with friends/family members who encourage participation in activities that interest them, such as hobbies or talents, which could result in positive experiences shaping a better outlook on life moving forward.

Seeking expert intervention from therapists specializing in family therapy may be necessary if emotional trauma is observed - such treatments could help your kid(s) cope better by teaching coping mechanisms alongside practical communication skills needed for effective co-parenting strategies after separation/divorce recommended.

When parents separate or divorce creating a parenting plan that thoroughly addresses kids' emotional and physical well-being is vital.

By maintaining consistency across both households, you can help minimize disruption while supporting their sense of security during what could otherwise be a turbulent time. There's no denying that significant changes can be incredibly taxing on young minds - moving homes or schools being just two examples.

As you prepare your kids for these transitions, it's essential to keep explanations age-appropriate while making sure they know they still have access to caring support from parents.

At times like these, exercising empathy, patience, and commitment pays off when listening and understanding where your children are coming from. This practical advice can pave the way for helping your little ones heal and adjust positively while promoting overall emotional well-being. And remember - taking care of yourself is crucial in this process that requires so much dedication!

The following chapter delves deeper into practical strategies to rebuild and reconnect physically and emotionally after suffering betrayal. It teaches valuable tips on nurturing intimate relationships while promoting emotional honesty and creating a safe healing environment.

Please note that as you traverse this path of transformation, your efforts also extend to your children's happiness and well-being; rebuilding requires more than just the relationship between two partners.

Chapter 11: The Intimacy Dilemma: Rediscovering Physical Connection After Betrayal

Healing Wounds and Rebuilding Intimacy in the Aftermath of Betrayal:

Coming together physically again after unfaithfulness in any relationship can prove challenging for many reasons. This section delves into the typical worries that may arise while trying to rebuild a sense of closeness between you both after betrayal has been experienced.

From addressing concerns about opening up emotionally or trusting each other again - this stage can be difficult but is possible with careful consideration from both parties involved if they're willing to work together toward healing our wounds.

Encouraging Vulnerability While Rebuilding Physical Intimacy:

Rebuilding physical intimacy requires creating a safe space where partners feel comfortable expressing their needs without hesitation. For this purpose, you need openness and empathy towards each other's feelings.

We believe setting boundaries by establishing clear communication channels is essential so that both parties fully understand each other's needs. Together we will guide on expressing affectionate rather than intimidating ways that promote mutual satisfaction during recovery from hurtful events such as betrayal, ensuring meaningful relationships are built.

The path to regaining physical intimacy with your partner after experiencing betrayal can be filled with obstacles and uncertainties. However, adopting an attitude of self-compassion and patience can go a long way in creating an environment conducive to growth and healing.

Open communication is crucial in rebuilding physical intimacy as one explores desires while setting clear boundaries and respectfully listening to their partner's preferences.

We have discussed several aspects of initiating conversations about intimacy expressing needs, and wanting to maintain boundaries through consent seeking while sensitively recognizing the partners' vulnerabilities.

Rediscovering physical intimacy requires ongoing communication that supports exposure by addressing fears and seeking tools for connection while fostering safety and support; all contribute significantly towards restoring trust between partners after infidelity.

Mutual satisfaction and emotional healing should remain at the forefront during this process.

When trying to rebuild physical contact after experiencing betrayal navigating the complexities can be difficult without guidance, support, and practical advice, which is where Chapter 11 comes in - providing helpful tips on how best to approach this journey successfully by focusing on emotional healing, vulnerability and strategies that prioritize these.

Patience is crucial throughout this journey since rediscovering physical intimacy means addressing wounds caused by betrayal, which can be challenging. Potential emotional barriers include trust issues, fear of vulnerability - lingering pain from past experiences, etc. Hence open communication between partners becomes crucial to express their desires, boundaries, and concerns and having supportive dialogue in a safe space.

Emotional healing should always be prioritized since physical interactions aren't enough - true intimacy requires nurturing emotions, including trust and vulnerability, which form its foundation.

It would be best to guide yourself through cultivating empathy, compassion, and active listening, amongst other things, while encouraging acknowledgment and validation between both partners creating an environment adaptable for mutual understanding and growth.

Building trust remains central to re-establishing the physical connection between two people since it forms the basis for all relationships. Without it, any true intimacy cannot exist.

Betrayal can cause severe damage that takes considerable effort to repair if one wishes to rebuild faith in others. Honoring commitments demonstrating accountability, reliability, and authentic apologies are effective strategies for rebuilding trust, albeit with patience, as it takes time.

Each couple faces unique challenges regarding physical intimacy; therefore, Chapter 11 provides practical guidance on how partners can create a secure environment for sensual exploration while remaining mindful of each other's emotional needs.

For couples' relationships' foundations to be sustainable towards stronger connections, they should approach physical touch with a curious yet open-minded attitude toward each other while adapting accordingly over time.

REDISCOVERING COUPLE PHYSICAL CONNECTION POST-BETRAYAL:

After experiencing betrayal in a relationship, finding a physical connection once again can feel daunting. However, recognizing that intimacy is essential for building a healthy relationship is vital to rebuilding trust and emotional bonds. Remember that exercise of physicality requires time, effort, and patience.

For couples looking to rediscover their physical connection post-betrayal, prioritize open dialogue as the initial step. Start by having an honest discussion about your apprehensions surrounding your personal needs and relationship expectations without being judgmental towards one another – yet keeping honesty at the fore of everything.

Instead of assigning blame or bringing up past mistakes, collaboratively set new benchmarks for one another moving forward while practicing understanding regarding one another's healing timelines.

At times like these, it's essential to understand that individuals heal at their own pace after betrayal; it's crucial to allow adequate time for recovery without undue pressure being applied. To complement open communication between partners, seeking expert help may be a wise option for regaining physical intimacy.

A qualified therapist can offer valuable guidance and support and identify underlying emotional challenges hindering the rebuilding process from betrayal. Moreover, creating a safe space for physical intimacy demands setting boundaries and establishing trust and mutual respect between partners.

Before engaging in sexual activity, it is paramount that couples prioritize building an emotional connection which they can accomplish by spending quality time together and taking part in shared activities that deepen personal insights through meaningful conversations.

Additionally, honoring individual desires while respecting each other's boundaries is vital for successfully rediscovering physical intimacy. Effective communication in expressing needs ensures both parties are comfortable and open-minded about necessary adjustments. Rediscovering physical intimacy after experiencing betrayal demands a curious approach full of exploration.

Couples must develop something novel and robust rather than trying to recapture what was lost. This may involve venturing into unknown territory by attempting new activities or experimenting with varying physical connection methods. Ultimately, this process requires much patience from both parties and regular communication that is always open and honest.

Couples seeking success in this area should prioritize creating a secure environment for the act while simultaneously making time to fully comprehend each other's desires and limits so they can approach intimacy in a way that feels agreeable for both partners.

REDISCOVERING ONE'S BODY AND DESIRES IN CASE THE RELATIONSHIP ENDS:

Rebuilding intimacy post-separation following the decision not to reconcile can be challenging for couples that have parted ways. Therefore we offer these five practical/psychological tips that may aid in restoring one's confidence:

Grant yourself enough time/space for processing emotions- ignoring feelings impedes progress.

Prioritize self-care—exercise/eat well/receive adequate rest while engaging in enjoyable activities like reading or bathing.

If struggling with low self-esteem/anxiety/depression seeking guidance from a qualified therapist/counselor may assist in developing healthy coping mechanisms.

Rediscover yourself- take ample time exploring your body better while discovering new desires along the way. Involvement in sports or physical activities positively impacts confidence levels alongside improving one's appearance – this ultimately translates into enhanced intimate experiences with partners.

Regular participation in exercise leads to increased blood circulation while elevating endorphin hormone production, thus enhancing stamina essential for fun-filled moments of passion between consenting adults!

To add more details about specific exercises, Kegels set a foundation by working on the pelvic muscles aiding bladder control while fostering strength in areas linked with arousal.

Hip and glute muscles are targeted explicitly during squats and lunges, essential for various positions requiring specific movements. Planks and core exercises contribute to a longer-lasting engagement during sex and support endurance classes more significantly.

Aerobic activities, such as running or swimming, boost cardiovascular health, improving stamina during sexual activity. The benefits of regular physical activity extend beyond just our physical health--it also improves body image and overall well-being, positively impacting our intimate encounters.

When entering into a new relationship after past setbacks or traumas, it is vital to openly communicate your story for trust-building measures alongside healthy boundary-setting strategies.

Building intimacy takes time; be sure you're patient with yourself while not hesitating to seek support or guidance as needed! Instead of dwelling on the past, strive forward by developing a more robust self-relationship.

Finally, Chapter 12 tackles the issue of dealing with deceit - an inevitable component of betrayal that frequently leads individuals who have experienced this type of trauma to grapple with uncertainty about truthfulness. Navigating deceit is tough—Chapter 12 discusses the challenges in rebuilding trust after someone has been dishonest. We explore common patterns of lying and guide how to address ongoing issues within your relationship.

The following chapter will delve deeper into recognizing deception and developing strategies for repairing trust over time.

Remember: building physical intimacy requires a strong foundation of mutual trust, emotional healing from past hurts, and open communication all along the way.

Chapter 12: Trust Lost, Truth Elusive: Dealing with Deceit and Patterns of Dishonesty

Breaking Free from the Cycle of Lies and Deception

Infidelity can shake the foundation of any relationship, causing mistrust that needs rebuilding for things to move forward positively. This chapter, tailored explicitly for that buying, offers practical advice regarding deciphering the deceptive tendencies within romantic partnerships while offering constructive strategies toward restoring transparency, truthfulness, and integrity within these relationships.

Identifying deceptive patterns is essential in breaking free from them and beginning the healing process in your relationship. We discuss how lying manifests itself through conflicting stories or information withholding, thus making it easier to recognize these tendencies when they arise; addressing them promptly prevents any potential escalation further down the line.

Observing behavioral cues and patterns that suggest deception is critical to recognize whether a partner is not telling the truth. Consider employing these practical guidelines to assist in identifying lying behavior:

1. Observe body language: Those lying often display particular physical cues like avoiding eye contact, fidgeting, or shifting weight from one foot to the other. Tense defensive posturing, like crossed arms, is also typical.

2. Listen closely for speech patterns: Liars may speak slowly or haltingly and repeat phrases or words to gain time or distract others. They may also use a higher-pitched tone than usual.

3. Look for signs of distress: Lies frequently produce signs of nervousness, such as sweating, blushing, and shallow breathing

4. Be alert for inconsistencies: Lies usually have contradictions in their details, providing clues that may reveal deceit.

5. Trust your intuition: When sensing deception, sometimes following your instincts is the best option, even if you can't identify a suspicious cue or behavior. Sometimes identifying falsehoods can be tricky, especially when dealing with someone close like your spouse.

However, there are various techniques available that can help highlight inconsistencies in their behavior and verbal communication patterns.

One such approach is asking open-ended questions instead of closed yes or no ones; this tactic leads your spouse to elaborate more on their claims and intricacies of their story, thus making it difficult for them to perpetuate their lies.

Additionally, spotting microexpressions also plays an essential role in detecting lies. These quick facial expressions reflect underlying emotions one tries hard not to show or control during lying instances. Recognizing these subtle cues accurately requires practice, but once mastered gives invaluable insights into where falsehoods exist.

Thus identifying micro expressions such as fake smiling indicating discomfort/insecurity, furrowed brows denoting confusion/frustration/disapproval helps one ascertain the genuineness of the individual's words and intent, further supported by tight-lipped expressions reflective of anger/frustration and wide eyes displaying surprise/shock.

Another example is when an individual looks down to the right while pointing towards a brewing concoction of lies and fabrication. Identifying lying behavior in a spouse is no easy feat; however, specific physical indicators can help you discern whether they may engage in deception.

Squinting eyes could indicate sadness or insecurity while biting one's lips suggests nervousness or anxiety. Similarly, touching the nose and face could signify an attempt at camouflage or discomfort.

Moreover, recognizing patterns is vital - if repeated lies were uttered previously by one's partner, chances are a specific modus operandi has been established while lying, which needs identification upon reoccurrence.

Defensiveness, when queried upon suspicious incidents, should not go unnoticed since it hints at an effort to hide something significant.

If detecting signs of dishonesty proves difficult despite attempts, then seeking professional help such as therapy from a qualified counselor shouldn't seem far-fetched since having trained staff by one's side makes things easier.

Behavioral cues coupled with trusting one's instincts are crucial to sharpening the ability to catch lies in a partner.

It's essential to remember that deceitfulness may signal underlying concerns within a relationship, and tackling these concerns is crucial for restoring confidence and reconstructing the connection.

Building trust necessitates a strong will toward fostering transparency between all parties involved, effectively cultivating honest communication that instills confidence over time. I offered you valuable tips such as sharing access codes or monitoring individual whereabouts, amongst other helpful ideas, to create more open dialogue during conversations and discussions.

Establishing trust after experiencing deceit is challenging but necessary work. A crucial element of this process is implementing mechanisms for accountability that prioritize transparency between both partners.

Couples can rebuild a deep sense of mutual trust by setting clear boundaries defining consequences for dishonesty, and regularly checking in with one another about how well they're being honest.

Moreover, by committing themselves fully to transparent behavior with each other—couples can embrace honesty as the foundation for building a more robust partnership. Betrayal can shatter trust in relationships leaving both partners feeling lost and uncertain about their future together.

Chapter 12 delves into the profound impact that deceitful behavior can have on relationships - offering guidance on navigating through these difficult times with practical advice and strategies for rebuilding trust. This chapter helps you understand the dynamics of deception by exploring different forms that dishonesty could take, from outright lies to omissions or half-truths - equipping you with tools to recognize patterns that may have emerged.

Dealing with deception can be challenging, but fostering an environment where open communication is encouraged can help facilitate honesty between partners.

Creating a space where both parties feel comfortable sharing their thoughts without fearing retribution or judgment can pave the way toward transparency and healing.

This chapter aims to guide readers through difficult conversations by encouraging active listening from both sides while highlighting empathy and understanding. This promotes confronting patterns of dishonesty head-on for one to seek clarity and truth, thus enabling moving forward.

Another vital aspect in rebuilding trust after deception is setting limits and establishing clear expectations on how one desires their relationships should look now, moving forward from present-day circumstances.

Exploring what edges must be defined and put into place as a boundary measure allows self-protection while preserving the relationship from further harm. It emphasizes the importance of both parties accepting responsibility for their actions while working consciously to rebuild trust. Establishing a framework that promotes honesty, integrity, and accountability within the dynamics is essential.

Near the end of Chapter 12, I want to encourage you to brace yourself for a concluding section called "Embracing Your Path to Healing."

This last chapter echoes the transformative journey undertaken thus far by readers and explores the growth experienced during this process while exploring possibilities that lie ahead. As you recover from infidelity in your relationships or marriage, it's vital not to lose hope; instead, embrace resilience!

The concluding chapter serves up inspiration that will help strengthen perseverance towards healing with adequate love for oneself through seeking out essential aspects like reflection and compassion during challenging times ahead - no matter how difficult they appear today!

Empowerment awaits those who are willing because assignment brings forth possibilities! While guiding readers through transformational journeys filled with growth and healing experiences coupled with lessons learned, therein comes an exclusive bonus chapter on managing financial matters post-divorce, as I fully understand the weight of financial implications in decisions to dissolve relationships.

Let's delve into some crucial aspects like dividing assets, managing debts, establishing financial independence, and protecting your economic welfare during one of life's most challenging seasons: divorce.

The key is mastering the financial terrain while making informed decisions to secure our future while laying the foundation for a fresh start filled with renewed hope. This chapter seeks to empower you by guiding how to take control of your finances regardless of whether professional assistance is required; practical solutions will be offered too, which make light work out of worries/uncertainties often linked with managing money post-divorce.

Always remember that there is strength in numbers - I am right beside you every step of the way! You have all it takes - the tools (knowledge) required to arrive at wise financial decisions imbued with confidence and optimism, irrespective of how thorny it might seem presently or in the future between all parties involved in a divorce situation.

Here lies a valuable resource that provides immense value while navigating through the complexities of divorce.

Let's empower ourselves together as we establish a solid financial foundation for a brighter tomorrow.

As you conclude this final chapter, remember your immense strength and resilience. Dealing with infidelity requires tremendous determination- fortunately for readers like yourself, practical advice, insights, and strategies have been compiled within this helpful guidebook designed for navigating such complexities while recovering from such trying circumstances successfully.

My intentions were simple: provide as much support and guidance as possible, thus propelling readers towards healing and rebuilding their lives following such trauma caused by infidelity.

As our resource draws to a close, indulge yourself with an appreciation for its contents and acknowledge the time invested in creating said guide- we guarantee it will leave a lasting impact once read until completion leaving readers more prone towards taking action than before while applying their newly acquired knowledge to their own life.

I hope this experience was insightful, uplifting, and instrumental in rebuilding trust.

SPECIAL BONUS CHAPTER:

Managing the Financial Aspects after Divorce: Navigating a New Financial Landscape

Divorce can bring significant emotional and financial changes that require careful consideration and planning.

By taking proactive steps and seeking professional help, you can confidently navigate this new economic landscape and secure your future after a divorce.

To manage finances effectively after a divorce, consider these suggestions:

Assess Your Financial Situation: Examine all relevant documents, such as tax returns, bank statements, and investment portfolios, to understand your assets, liabilities, and shared obligations within the current economic climate.

Seek Sound Advice: Consult with qualified lawyers specializing in family law or trusted financial advisors knowledgeable in these situations who will guide you through complex issues such as asset division or spousal support while keeping future interests safe. Creating a Budget and Addressing Property Division and Retirement Planning after Divorce

After a divorce, *adjusting to a new financial reality is essential.*

One crucial step is creating a post-divorce budget that aligns with your circumstances. This involves evaluating your income, expenses, and financial goals and prioritizing your needs while making necessary adjustments. A well-planned budget will provide clarity and help you make sound financial decisions.

Another significant aspect of divorce is *property division*. Working with your attorney to determine a fair distribution of assets, including real estate, vehicles, investments, and personal belongings, is essential.

It's necessary to consider the long-term implications of any agreements made and seek legal advice to protect your rights. Divorce may also impact your retirement plans.

You should evaluate joint retirement accounts, pensions, or other retirement assets and discuss the potential division or rollover options with your financial advisor. Then adjust your retirement strategy based on these changes in circumstances while seeking guidance on maximizing savings and investment opportunities.

Lastly, reviewing and updating estate planning documents such as wills, trusts, and beneficiary designations after divorce is crucial. This allows you to ensure that all decisions are up to date with the current situation.

Going through a divorce can be draining both financially and emotionally but taking care of financial matters properly will ease some pressure later on--make sure your assets go to the people or causes that align with your wishes and choose individuals who will handle any essential financial or healthcare matters competently.

In addition, build an emergency fund as insurance against unanticipated expenses which may come up; this safety net should cover costs for three to six months.

If the split led to income loss or instability, consider looking into new job opportunities or developing skills further--the result could lead to more earnings for you in the long run.

Finally, don't forget about the impact of divorce on credit scores: take control by closing joint accounts ASAP and frequently review reports for any inaccuracies; having solid credit opens many doors toward different kinds of lucrative investments and loans later on.

The aftermath of a divorce can cause stress from immediate concerns and stable future economic security, which should be addressed promptly.

Achieving financial happiness requires skills such as identifying wise investment options, saving for retirement plans, and setting reasonable goals aligned with one's values.

The process might seem intimidating, but a careful, planned approach coupled with professional guidance is the key to helping navigate this transition and providing an opportunity for a new beginning.

Also, after a divorce, it's essential to manage debts responsibly. Creating a feasible plan helps prioritize loans with the highest interest rates while considering restructuring.

If possible, avoid new financial obligations and focus on spending habits to maintain financial stability. Don't let a divorce derail your finances - take proactive steps to safeguard yourself against potential economic impacts.

Begin by reviewing all of your insurance options: health insurance coverage for both you and any dependents you have may need adjustment; similarly, ensure any life or property-based policies still cover those who matter most to you after the split.

It's also vital that you understand how any changes brought about by the impending settlement could lead to changes in taxes owed after the split; seek guidance from experts such as tax professionals if unsure.

If children are involved in any way during proceedings - either directly or via payments such as child support - *it is vital that all parties consider long-term expenses* such as college tuition or healthcare costs after splitting assets throughout the proceedings, if possible via trusts or other means which protect everyone involved from future anxieties about payment plans falling through.

Ultimately divorce often leads to a period of transition and adjustment. One of the most significant changes can be newfound financial independence; embrace this time for growth and self-sufficiency by developing your financial knowledge and skills through research, courses, or other means.

Financial stability requires learning about investments, retirement planning, and other essential financial matters. You can participate in financial literacy programs or seek professional help to establish a stable financial foundation.

The reality is that handling finances during a divorce can be emotionally exhausting. Don't hesitate to ask for assistance from your social network, such as friends, family, or support groups; your emotional well-being is directly connected with your finances.

Building a solid support system will give you the encouragement and resilience you require throughout this transformational period. Remember that every individual's experience with divorce differs; thus, there isn't an all-encompassing approach to managing the financial aspect of it all.

Be sure to tailor these suggestions according to your specific situation while consulting professionals capable of providing personalized advice so you can confidently take charge of your finances using informed decision-making skills while embracing newfound independence. Handling the monetary aspects after a divorce shouldn't merely be about surviving but thriving!

You have an unparalleled moment to redefine your financial ambitions by emphasizing personal well-being. Take small steps towards securing more excellent stability in all areas of life so that hope is not lost within challenging moments but strengthened by them.

Believe steadfastly in yourself as someone capable of achieving great things- regardless of how daunting they may seem- because ultimately, through hard work, anything is possible when we set our minds to it!

SECOND BONUS CHAPTER:

WHAT TO DO WHEN IT'S TIME TO WALK AWAY AFTER AFFAIR

Embarking on life after ending an affair is unsettling; however, taking preemptive measures ensures that you're looking after yourself. Here are some constructive tips to bear in mind:

Seek support: Identifying individuals with whom you can confide is crucial - whether it be trusted family/friends or attending a support group for infidelity survivors.

Take control of finances: Financial autonomy is paramount following a separation when married or in a domestic partnership. Open an independent bank account gather savings for future purposes, and consult with a legal professional on your rights and legal options. 3.

Prepare an action plan: Draft a course for transitioning into new living arrangements, including finding suitable accommodation securing employment, and arranging any necessary childcare - all while creating small daily targets to monitor progress.

When deciding to end an unhealthy relationship, it's critical to prioritize self-care work. Walking away can trigger intense emotional upheaval – ensure you're managing stressors by maintaining healthy habits like eating well-balanced diets incorporating regular exercise into your routine and getting consistently restful sleep cycles each night. Counseling services can also be beneficial when working through complex emotions resulting from relationship dissolution.

Whenever viable, it's advisable to minimize interaction with former romantic partners during the initial stages of adjustment anchoring recovery processes after leaving an affair situation. Stepping out of problems like these creates opportunities for self-exploration- accounting for potential growth via new endeavors such as joining clubs or pursuing hobbies that align with passions will help rediscover what drives you while creating a new sense of identity.

Remember, making brave choices prioritizing one's safety and well-being indicates empowerment. Keep focused on goals, exhibit kindness to yourself during this challenging period, and consider steps that guarantee well-being.

YOUR FUTURE WITHOUT HELP FROM YOUR PARTNER

Losing your partner can leave you feeling lost when managing daily tasks they once handled efficiently. Recognize that it's natural not knowing everything and that seeking assistance is helpful. Here are three practical tips for finding help:

Explore online resources: The vast array of tutorials, articles, or videos available on the web can offer step-by-step guidance in almost every area imaginable, including cooking and home improvement sites such as YouTube, eHow, or Wikihow ventures would be worth considering in gaining knowledge about specific areas.

Rely on close family members or friends for assistance - it takes just one call! : It isn't wrong asking someone you trust for their opinion/service even if they aren't experienced professionals- most people will be happy helping out a loved one.

Consider seeking professional assistance: Professional services such as counseling or therapy could prove helpful and supportive during this challenging period. If you seek personal growth, participating in workshops or classes provided by community centers or libraries could be just the thing for you!

Learning practical skills like cooking, home maintenance, or financial planning through these events enhances self-sufficiency and drives social interaction with like-minded individuals too! Even though learning something new isn't always easy, it shouldn't deter you from trying it - all it takes is persistence and the willingness to improve oneself over time for fruitful results!

Moving forward positively is possible with practical steps towards safety and self-care post affair.

Taking proactive measures such as seeking emotional support from those closest to you, stabilizing your finances for added security, formulating an effective strategy for moving forward, and putting self-care at the forefront are vital components in navigating this transitional period.

Cutting off contact with negative influences is essential in embracing new experiences and fostering positivity.

Conclusion: Embracing Your Path to Healing

Reflecting on this transformative journey as we wrap up this book is essential. It's crucial to appreciate how much effort it took to confront pain head-on while navigating infidelity, rebuilding trust, and finding yourself again.

Your dedication to seeking guidance throughout has proven how much personal growth means to you. In light of any adversities faced along the way, it's clear that empowerment through positive change is in your future mindset now more than ever!

Being kind to yourself by practicing self-love, self-care, and self-compassion should be a priority in life. Building meaningful connections with others created from trustful bonds and open communication leads towards empowerment while feeling genuinely fulfilled!

Before anything else, though, let me start by saying thank you so much for selecting this book to guide you in your journey of mending after infidelity!

Your dedication to the solutions mentioned throughout these chapters has not gone unnoticed, and I feel it's important to acknowledge that!

You are now equipped with valuable tools to help overcome obstacles and capitalize on opportunities throughout your path! While focusing on healing emotionally, if you're going through a divorce due to infidelity, take time to manage financial aspects and seek advice from professionals like financial advisors or attorneys to secure your future by understanding your rights, responsibilities, and options. Setting off on a new chapter in life requires adequate financial stability for overall wellness.

From our discussions in this book, maintaining positivity and motivation remains paramount.

It would be best to keep close contacts who offer support, such as family members or friends who can provide guidance with empathy or present an experienced ear during tough times while reminding you of your capability.

Self-care practices should always come first; hence, one must take time out conscientiously for emotional growth by practicing self-compassion daily. Continually improving oneself by developing new interests or hobbies that bring joy into their life is fundamental to building momentum towards successively embracing a positive mindset and creating an environment full of love, trust, and true happiness reignition.

I want to conclude by expressing my most profound gratitude for choosing our book as your companion during these times of anticipating healing.

It has been an honor providing you with the right direction while lending the necessary support throughout these pages.

Please remember, this process requires a resilient spirit that overcomes challenges and hurdles that come with visible optimism because in you lies great strength capable of surmounting any obstacle.

Embrace your journey towards healing with confidence in yourself – know that it's possible to manifest a future drenched in love-filled relationships founded on trust. You're one of a kind, so naturally, it's up to you alone, yet I have faith in the power of which you're capable of achieving true satisfaction and internal peace.

Blair Parker

Made in United States
North Haven, CT
17 August 2023

40420513R00095